M *is for* MACKINAC

A NATURE ALPHABET

By Katy Klimczuk
Illustrated by Kate Dupre

Copyright © 2023 Katy Klimczuk
All world rights reserved.

No part of this book may be reproduced, stored in a retrieval system, or transmitted in any form or by any means electronic, mechanical, photocopying, recording or otherwise, without the prior consent of the publisher.

Readers are encouraged to go to www.MissionPointPress.com to contact the author or to find information on how to buy this book in bulk at a discounted rate.

Published by Mission Point Press
2554 Chandler Rd.
Traverse City, MI 49696
(231) 421-9513
www.MissionPointPress.com

ISBN: 978-1-958363-68-3
Printed in the United States of America

A is for ARCH ROCK

*An upside-down U with a wonderful view
Curving up high, in the clear blue sky.*

Arch Rock is made of limestone and was formed by the disappearing waters of an ancient lake thousands of years ago. There are only a handful of arches in Michigan, which makes it rare and special. Look for the small cedar trees growing on top!

B is for BUTTERFLY

*Delicate wings flutter in orange and in black
From Mexico to Mackinac and all the way back.*

Mackinac Island is a seasonal home to monarch butterflies. Their caterpillars feed on milkweed plants in the island's meadows. Take a look near the east end of Mackinac Island Airport late in the summer to see monarchs preparing for their long flight south to Mexico for the winter.

C is for CRACK IN THE ISLAND

*Deep in the island and way out back
A break in the Earth forms a big crack!*

You can actually tuck yourself into the gap in the ground called Crack in the Island. It always makes for a fun photo! Legend says that Gitchi Manitou, or the Great Spirit, stomped this crack in the ground.

D is for DEVIL'S KITCHEN

Circle the island and on your way south
Stop by the cave with an open mouth.

Devil's Kitchen is another spectacular limestone formation on the island.
Shaped by waves over thousands of years, it looks like a face with an open mouth.
Its blackened inside likely comes from fires built long ago.

E is for EAGLE POINT CAVE

*Up a steep hill and not very wide
Eagle Point Cave makes a great place to hide.*

You can find Eagle Point Cave on the north side of the island by hiking
up the Tranquil Bluff Trail. It was formed by erosion caused by waves.
See how many people you can squeeze inside!

F is for FORGET-ME-NOT

A dainty flower, so lovely to see
Provides nectar for the island honeybee.

Forget-me-nots are small, sky blue flowers that can be found blooming in the spring shade along trails in the forest. These small flowers spread quickly and can carpet the forest floor. They attract bees, ladybugs, and butterflies, among other pollinators.

G is for GERANIUMS

Geraniums pop in candy apple red
Planted in pots or sprawled in a bed.

Geraniums have been a part of Mackinac Island for over 100 years. They can bloom as early as spring and last into fall. They are a hardy flower that can handle cool temperatures. Geraniums brighten up the island and look vibrant against the crisp white of Mackinac's Grand Hotel.

H is for HORSES

Early in the morning, when you open the door
You will hear hoofs beating – one, two, three, four.

Without cars, you can get around the island
on bike, foot, or with the help of horses.
Over 500 horses come to the island each summer.
They give tours of the island, make deliveries,
and take visitors on trail rides.

I is for ISLAND

Mackinac is an island, surrounded by blue
In between the peninsulas two.

Mackinac Island is surrounded by Lake Huron. You can reach the island by ferry boat from either the Lower or Upper Peninsula. Thousands of years ago, Indigenous people settled on Mackinac and used it as a place to fish, hunt, and live.

J *is for* JACK-IN-THE-PULPIT

In the misty morning dew
This flower shouts out peek-a-boo.

Late in the spring and deep in the forest, you can search for jack-in-the-pulpit flowers. Look for the folded petal and the peek-a-boo stalk that make this flower unique.

K *is for* KNOTS IN TREES

A knot, or burl, shows the history
Of each island's special paper birch tree.

A knot in a tree is like a scar, sealing up a wound. They are important to the tree's survival and show how tough a tree can be. Explore the island to find paper birch trees with their signature thin white bark and see how many knots you can find!

L is for LILACS

The lilacs' fragrance, so strong and sweet
Scents the island in the sun and heat.

Lilacs' beautiful blooms bring lots of visitors at the beginning of each summer. They have been thriving on the island for over 200 years. You can find them all around Mackinac, especially at Marquette Park, which has over 75 species in bloom!

M is for MACKINAC

When glaciers melted many years ago
A turtle-shaped island rose from below.

N is for NORTHERN LIGHTS

*Look up to the heavens on a chilly night
And you may see the sky dancing so bright!*

Mackinac is the perfect place to see the northern lights – or aurora borealis – lighting up the night sky, especially in the fall and early spring. They may appear white, gray, or green to your eyes!

O is for OWL

Winter, spring, summer, or fall
Listen for a hooting call.

Most of the island is made up of protected land that owls can call home. They live in the forest along with rabbits, deer, coyotes, and other wildlife. You may spot a barred owl any time of the year or a snowy owl in the winter. *Hoo hoo*!

P is for PONTIAC TRAIL

High on West Bluff you will find this trail
Watch for ferries or boats with a sail.

Mackinac Island is 80 percent state park. Its protected land includes over 70 miles of trails. Walk the narrow Pontiac Trail along the island's southwest coast and wave to the Mackinac Bridge and boats below!

Q is for QUEEN ANNE'S LACE

*This delicate flower is a beautiful sight
Whose petals are patterned and blossoms so white.*

Queen Anne's Lace is also known as Wild Carrot, Bird's-Nest, and Bee's Nest-Plant. A nonnative wildflower, Queen Anne's Lace blooms in the summer and has detailed patterns that make it very unique. They look like mini firework explosions!

R is for RED-BELLIED WOODPECKER

This bird can be heard drumming high in a tree
With striped tail feathers and a crown of red to see.

Red-bellied woodpeckers may be heard before they're seen. Listen for the *kwirr* sound or the drumming on a tree. Despite its name, it can be very hard to spot the red on this woodpecker's belly. Instead, look for the bright red head!

S is for SUGAR LOAF

A soaring tower can be found
Seventy-five feet above the ground.

Tucked in the woods, surrounded by cedar trees, is a beautiful rock formation known as Sugar Loaf. It is made of limestone and soars high into the sky. Look closely and you may see the shape of a man's side profile in the rock.

T is for TRILLIUMS

Each spring, trilliums cover the forest floor
As Earth awakens and spreads flowers galore.

Blooming in May, trillium flowers are some of the first signs that spring has sprung on Mackinac Island. These large white wildflowers are a welcome sight after a long winter. Found in the forest, trilliums need to bloom early before the trees grow leaves and block their sunlight.

U is for UNDER THE STARS

After dark, the sky is sprinkled with stars.
Look for the Big Dipper, Milky Way, or Mars!

Mackinac Island has little light pollution. That means it gets dark enough to really see the beauty of our night skies. You may see stars, planets, or even a meteor shower when you gaze up at night.

V is for VIEWS

Magnificent views can be found up high
Standing above, what can you spy?

You can find beautiful views all around the island.
Watch the hustle and bustle from a distance at Anne's Tablet or catch
some peaceful lake views at Point Lookout or Sunset Rock.

W is for WILD BERRIES

Juicy berries in red, purple, and pink
Pluck one and taste – they're sweeter than you think.

You can find fresh berries growing on the island throughout the summer. Strawberries usually ripen in July, while raspberries and thimbleberries are available from July into September. Make sure you identify the berry before trying it!

X is for FOX

After the sun has set and the sky is dark
Listen for a red fox's howl or bark.

Although rare, you might spot a red fox on the island.
Try to stay up late to find one since these sly animals are nocturnal.
You might hear its bark or scream before you see one!

Y is for YELLOW LADY'S SLIPPERS

Look for the last wildflower to bloom in spring
Shaped like a slipper with yellow coloring.

Lady's slippers look just like their name suggests – delicate ballerina slippers! When a bee climbs inside the slipper, it must go through a maze that takes the bee past the pollen sac and out through a tiny hole in the back. The pollen will stick to the bee and carry it on to the next plant.

Z is for ZINNIAS

*It feels like summer has really begun
When colorful zinnias stand tall in the sun.*

Ferry boats and horse-drawn drays deliver annual flowers to cottages and hotels to be planted each spring. Zinnias bloom all summer long. Their bright colors give a festive look to island gardens. In every day, month, and season, there is colorful, unique beauty to enjoy on Mackinac Island.

A NOTE ABOUT NATURE

Mackinac Island is a very special land and over 80 percent state park. With abundant nature and wildlife, there is so much to see and discover. While you are out hiking or biking, be sure to respect the nature around you. Here's a few tips to help keep the island clean and pristine.

Don't pick the flowers!
Wildflowers should be left untouched for all to appreciate and private gardens should be admired from afar.

Respect the animals
If you happen to encounter a wild island animal, notice it quietly, give it plenty of space, and leave the animal as you found it.

Honor the history
Many of the island's rock formations have been formed over several centuries. Respect the work that Mother Nature has done over the years.

BIBLIOGRAPHY

Adirondacks Forever Wild. Wildflowers of the Adirondacks: Queen Anne's Lace. https://wildadirondacks.org

Allen, Sue, personal communication, 2021-22.

American Bird Conservancy. Red-bellied Woodpecker. https://abcbirds.org

Anyplace America. Top Arches in Michigan. https://www.anyplaceamerica.com

Awesome Mitten. (2022, September 27).

Awesome Mitten's ULTIMATE Guide of When, Where, & How to See the Northern Lights in Michigan. https://www.awesomemitten.com

Bagnall, Kyle, personal communication, 2022.

Bird Advisors. Male vs Female Woodpecker – Picture ID Guide. https://www.birdadvisors.com

Dupre, Kate, personal communication, 2022.

Geocaching. (2008). Eagle Point Cave. https://www.geocaching.com

Mackinac Island Tourism Bureau. (2022). https://www.mackinacisland.org

Mackinac State Historic Parks. https://www.mackinacparks.com

Matheny, Keith. (2015, December 24). Can Mackinac milkweed help the monarchs? Detroit Free Press. https://www.freep.com

Monarch Joint Venture. (2022). https://monarchjointventure.org

The Natural Web. (2015) Yellow Lady's Slipper – Like Winning the Lottery. https://the-natural-web.org/

Pure Michigan. https://www.michigan.org

Robinson, John. (2019, August 27). The Legend of Mackinac's Crack-in-the-Island. https://99wfmk.com

Westfall, Jamie, personal communication, 2022. Wikipedia. Daucus carota. https://en.wikipedia.org

Wild Ambience. Red Fox Sounds & Calls. https://wildambience.com

Wohletz, Jennifer, personal communication, 2022.

ABOUT THE AUTHOR

Katy Klimczuk has degrees in both elementary education and reading and spent several years teaching. Becoming a children's book author was a natural next step. Katy's work has been published in Walloon Writers Review, Beanstack's 1000 Books Badge Book, and a handful of blogs. In addition to writing, she homeschools her children and hopes to pass along her love of learning, nature, and stories to young readers.

Katy is also a member and co-coordinator for her local SCBWI-Michigan group. She was married on Mackinac Island and enjoys frequent trips up north. She lives in Grosse Pointe Farms, Michigan, with her husband, two children, and two cats. Find out more at www.katyklimczuk.com.

ABOUT THE ILLUSTRATOR

Kate Dupre is a Mackinac Island resident who works both independently as an artist and as the owner, operator, and instructor of Watercolor Cafe (opened in 2019). Kate's primary artistic passions are watercolor and acrylic painting. Having studied graphic design for her bachelor's degree, Kate has crafted her process away from digital work and toward painted illustrations for branding and marketing purposes as well as custom commissions in fine art. This is her second book after Goodnight, Mackinac Bridge (2018). She is inspired by the beauty and spirituality of Mackinac and much of her personal artwork is an ode to the natural Island. See more at www.katecreates.work.

www.ingramcontent.com/pod-product-compliance
Lightning Source LLC
Chambersburg PA
CBHW041417010526
44107CB00016B/1197